T0405436

9780811877886

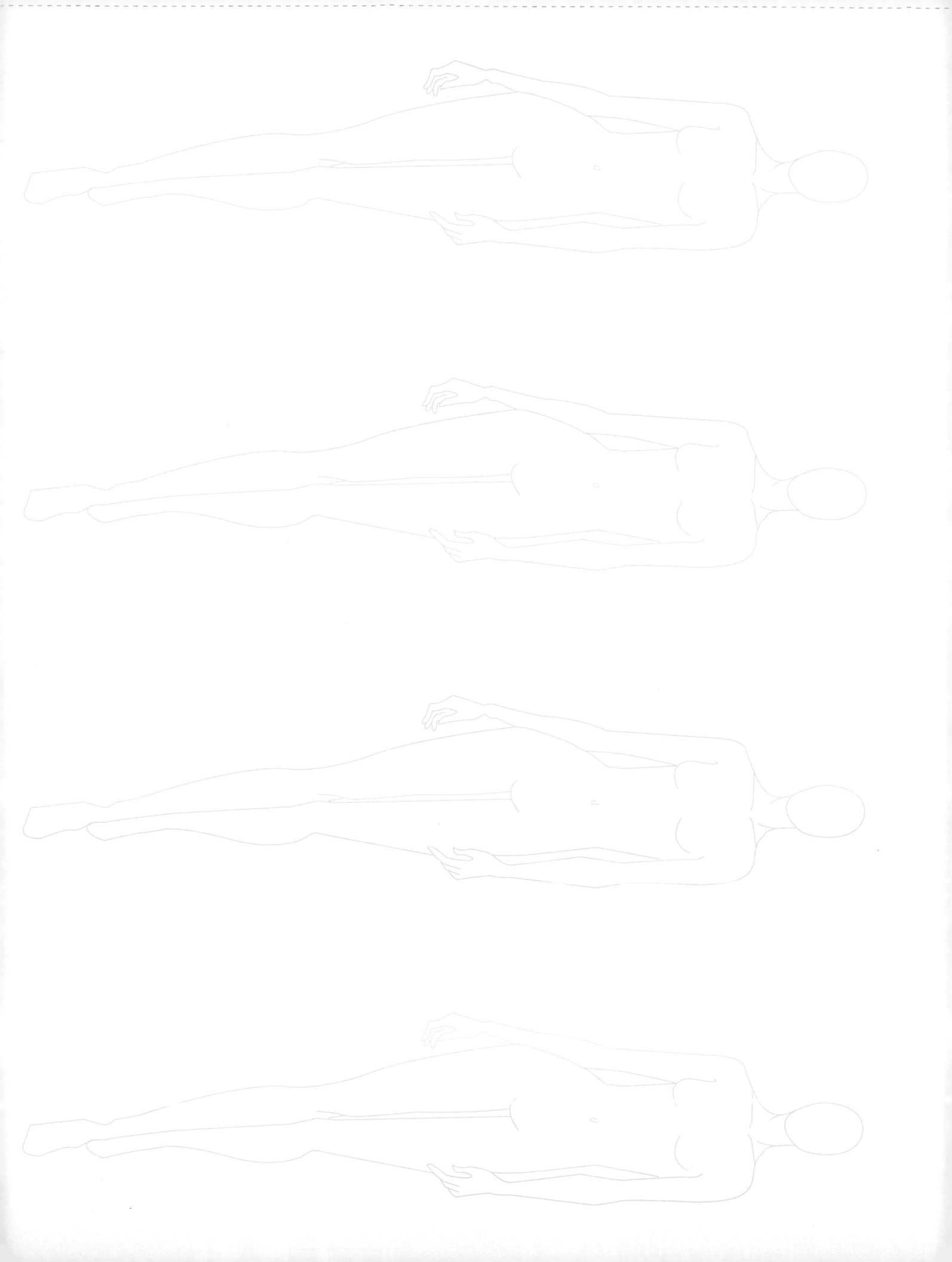

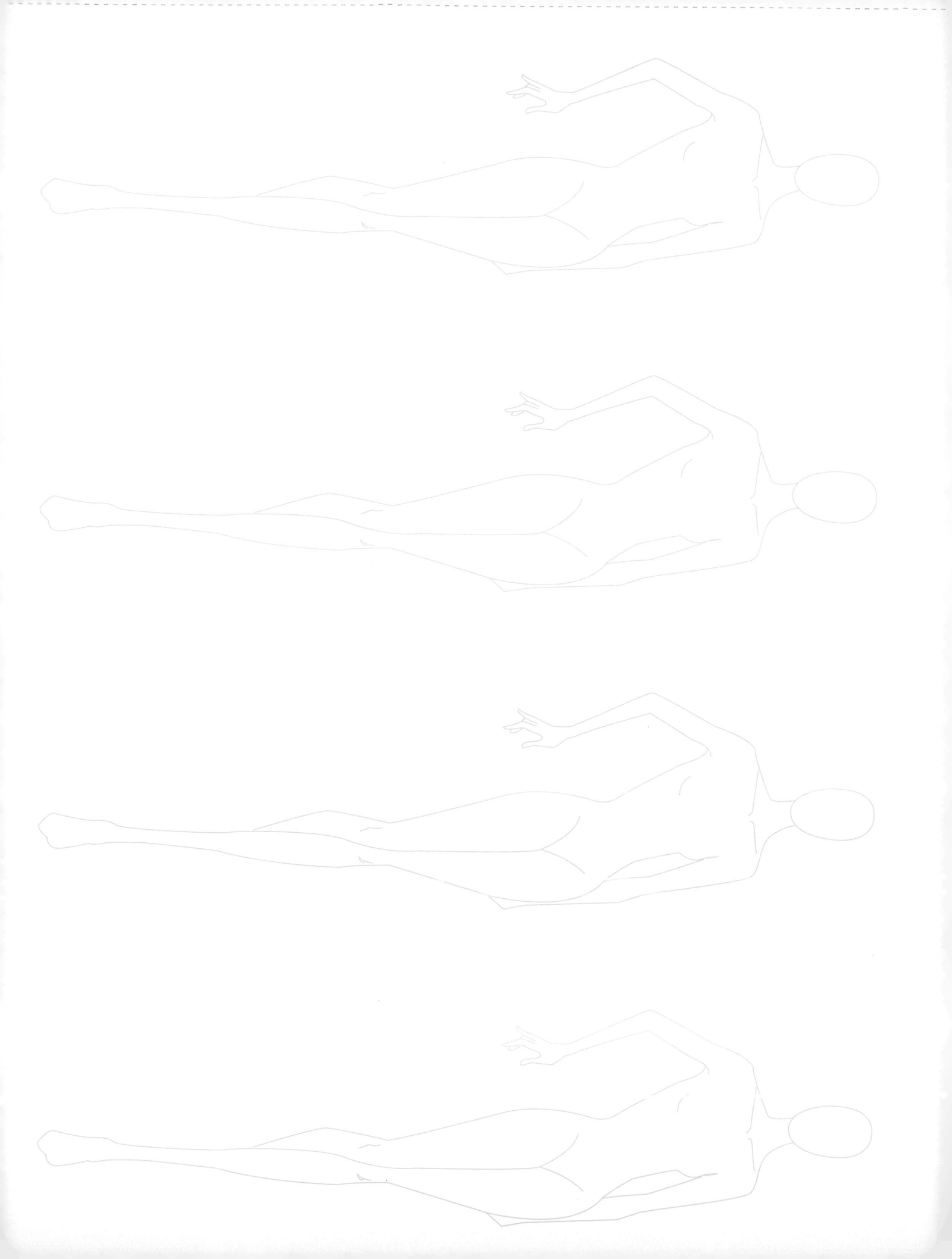

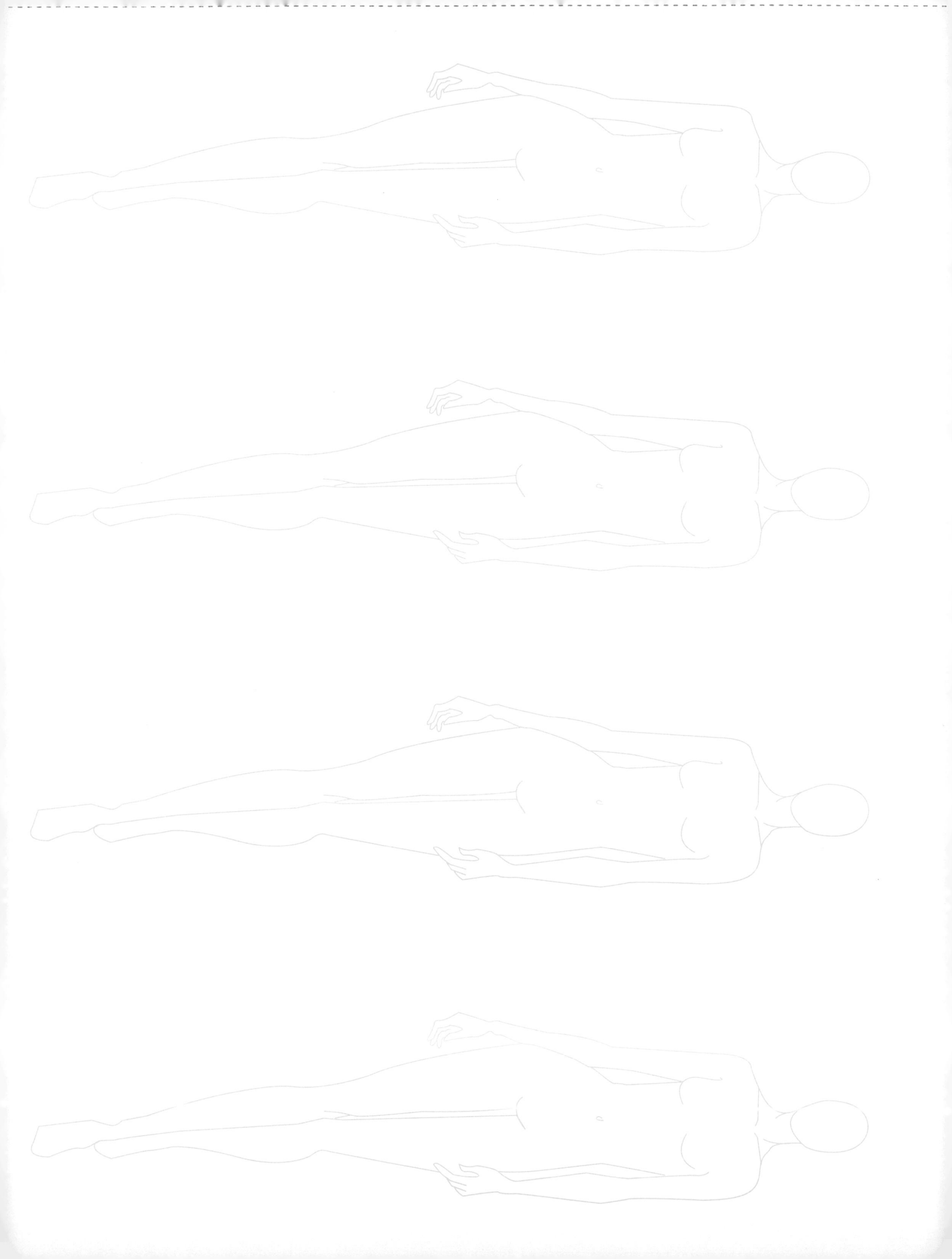

Recommended Reading

39th and Broadway
www.39thandbroadway.com
The vault of the fashion community. Here you'll find young hopefuls venting about the realities of their jobs in NYC and comparing experiences.

Apparel News
www.apparelnews.net
A news site so you can keep your finger on the pulse of the retail business.

Burda Style
www.burdastyle.com
Supportive and helpful online community of sewers and designers, plus an informative blog and fun giveaways.

The Business of Fashion
www.businessoffashion.com
Informed, analytical, and opinionated point of view on the fashion industry. Delivering fashion business intelligence on emerging designers, technologies, and global brands that are making their mark on the industry.

Coroflot
www.coroflot.com
Post your portfolio, check out other peoples' work, and find a job!

Designer's Nexus
www.designersnexus.com
Great free resources for experienced and novice designers. Includes downloads, tutorials, e-books, and articles.

Fashion Era
www.fashion-era.com
Fantastic for researching a specific period in fashion history. Don't be put off by the disheveled appearance; this site hosts myriad searchable articles organized by topic and time period.

Fashion Chalkboard
www.fashionchalkboard.com
Online training library plus CD- and DVD-based video training for creative designers, instructors, students, and hobbyists.

Fashion Club
www.fashionclub.com
Created by the Fashion Institute of Design and Merchandising (FIDM), Fashion Club is aimed at teens passionate about a career in fashion. The site helps aspiring designers set up clubs in their high schools, turning a hobby into a professional path. Includes contests, trend reports, and great tips on choosing your fashion major.

Fashion Students Online
www.fashionstudentsonline.com
A vibrant community of students, home learners, hobbyists, and even grannies who are interested in knowing how to do more than just sew. The blog entries are often informative and you'll pick up lots of good tips in the tutorials.

Pantone
www.pantone.com
Pantone is widely recognized as the international authority for color forecasting and standardizing colors across the spectrum. It's worth visiting their site periodically to stay in the know on the latest color trends and directions.

Pinky Shears
www.pinkyshears.com
Revealing interviews and honest articles that offer real insight into what it's like to work in the industry.

Simplicity.com
www.simplicity.com
Deals, tips, contests, and a useful store for picking up sewing supplies.

Style.com
www.style.com
Check out runway collections as soon as they are revealed, read critics' opinions of the season's trends, and see great detail shots of accessories, models, and after-parties.

UsTrendy
www.ustrendy.com
Gain exposure for your work and potentially win some cash! Post your portfolio on the site to enter design competitions and get valuable feedback on your designs.

WGSN
www.wgsn.com
Members-only site for trend forecasting and reporting from around the world.

Women's Wear Daily
www.wwd.com
A fashion authority for the business of style and fashion for its devoted readership. Women's Wear Daily is dedicated to the fashion, beauty, and retail industries, with timely, credible business news and key women's fashion trends.

Inspirational Reading

Beta Fashion
www.betafashion.com
Beta Fashion is a contemporary, print-focused women's fashion label. All Beta Fashion products are made in collaboration with a global community of designers. Here you can become part of that community and share your designs for a chance to learn from others and gain exposure.

Bobbin Talk
www.bobbintalk.com
Dedicated to promoting the creative force of emerging and independent designers. It features fashion and accessory collections, conceptual photography, fashion sketches, and illustrations from hand-picked young designers and college students. The blog is infused with the personal opinions and style musings of Aneta Genova, accessory designer, book author, and assistant professor of fashion at Parsons The New School for Design in New York.

Miss Capricho
www.misscapricho.com
Miss Capricho's breezy and whimsical fashion illustrations seamlessly portray the mood of an outfit. She is a great artist to watch, as she showcases a modern and playful manifestation of fashion illustration.

Paper Fashion
www.paperfashion.wordpress.com
This Chicago-based fashion designer's illustrations are lovely and inspiring. She updates her blog frequently and has occasional giveaways.

Polyvore
www.polyvore.com
Resources for putting together your own fashion spreads and mood boards. You can see how that hard-to-imagine clothing combo you've been wanting to try will look.

The Sartorialist
www.thesartorialist.blogspot.com
Daily posts of inspiring outfits put together by "real" people on the streets, spotted by globe-trotting fashion photographer Scott Schuman.

Sea of Shoes
www.seaofshoes.typepad.com
Click on over to this fashion blog to soak up the informed opinions on designer collections, photos of expensive heels, and wild styling by a Dallas suburbanite and her mother. The young Aldridge records her daily attire and avant-garde inspirations with jaw-dropping styling.

Style Bubble
www.stylebubble.typepad.com
Susie Lau's London-based blog assesses fresh local talent and showcases her daily experiments with careful clashes and considered mixes of cutting-edge designer gear. Style Bubble stands out thanks to the frequency of the posts, Susie's dedication, and the range and extent of her knowledge.

The Style Rookie
www.thestylerookie.com
A blog written by a very young and accomplished fashion writer. Tavi's fresh writing style and candid self-portraits always offer a new take on the fashion scene. Her adventurous explorations are admirable and her enthusiasm is contagious!

Industry Terms

Want to talk the talk?

Whether it's your first day on the job, you're interviewing at your dream fashion school, or you just want to sound like the pros, we've got your back. Tear off this little cheat sheet and keep it handy. You'll knock their yarn-dyed socks off!

Allover print: Often screen-printed, an allover print is composed of a design that is repeated across the entire surface of a garment.

Artwork: When designers talk about "artwork," they usually mean an embellishment or design detail such as a screen print, embroidery, beading, eyelet appliqué, or other decorative element.

CAD: Computer Aided Design refers to flats that have been drawn using Adobe Illustrator or similar software. Most designers initially sketch by hand, and then translate their sketches onto the computer to apply various fills and colors. Using CAD allows designers to quickly experiment with different colors and shapes resulting in fewer adjustments to samples. CADs are often used in place of actual samples to present the collection to the buyer.

Collection: A fashion collection is a group of styles that designers put together each season to showcase new trends. A season is usually defined as either autumn/winter or spring/summer. This will often include a percentage of classic styles that evolves slightly each year together with shorter term trendy products.

Color cards: Groupings of color used to communicate the theme or mood of a collection. Color standards are usually arranged in a row using Pantone chips, fabric swatches, paint, or anything else that relates just the right shade. Usually each tone has a name or reference code written next to it so it can be identified. Color cards can also be sent by a factory for easy reference.

Colorways: An array of colors that contrast and complement one another is chosen for apparel designs. These are prepared for stripes, prints, and solids.

Croquis: Figure templates used by fashion designers to ensure their garments come out proportional on the first try. Designers often trace croquis with tracing paper, or use them as a guide under their sketch paper.

Fits: During a fit session, a technical design team often consisting of a head designer, pattern maker, and technical designer measures a sample garment on a fit model. The garment is scrutinized to ensure that it lays properly and all the finishing details such as print placement, artwork placement, topstitching, and trim are finalized. Often, a junior assistant will take notes on the fit session to follow-up with the production team.

Flats: Flat sketches are the blueprints that specify how a garment is to be constructed. These are drawn by hand or using a computer (see CAD) as if the garment was laid flat, to display all the design details, including darts, hardware, print placement, artwork, and topstitching. An essential component of the design package, flats serve as the main method of communication between designer, patternmaker, factory, and buyer.

Garment dying: A popular dying technique in which a whole, finished garment is dipped in a dye bath and processed. This can be done at the last minute, ensuring the color is relevant to the up-to-the-minute trends. Garment dying also preshrinks the garment, which will help minimize customer returns.

Grades: Once the fit of a sample is approved, that garment will be graded up and down, meaning that a chart will be put together with the measurement adjustments necessary to process the style in a range of sizes.

Hand: Also called hand feel, the term *hand* refers to the quality and characteristics of fabrics that are perceived only by touching them. For example, firmness, softness, silkiness, drape, and stretch are ways to describe the hand feel of a garment.

Haute couture: French for "high sewing" or "high dressmaking," *haute couture* refers to custom, made-to-measure pieces that cost tens of thousands of dollars. In order to use the term, designers must have a Paris showroom; e.g, Christian Dior, Jean Paul Gaultier, Chanel, Givenchy.

Illustrations: Fashion illustrations are stylized drawings used to communicate the mood and spirit of a garment. An important tool for demonstrating a designers' flair and creativity, as well as sketching skills, these are nevertheless not often used in the industry due to time constraints.

Lab dips: Small swatches of fabric dyed by a factory to match a color standard requested by the designer or coloring team. Lab dips are essential in determining how a fabric will respond to a certain shade, though the color can still vary when dyed in bulk quantities.

Line sheets: Used by salespeople or designers to present a collection to buyers. The line sheet features a flat sketch or CAD of each style for a season, along with a style number, season, pricing information, color and fabric details, and delivery date. Sometimes they also contain actual fabric swatches.

Mood board: Collages of items such as photographs, sketches, magazine clippings, fabric swatches, trim samples, and color samples all strategically arranged on a board to communicate the spirit and theme of a collection.

Overdyed: When piece-dyed garments or yarn-dyed fabrics are put through an additional dye color in a process that creates unique shades.

Piece dye: Fabric that is dyed after it is woven or knitted. In piece dyeing, which is mainly used for fabrics that are to be a solid color, a continuous length of dry cloth is passed through a trough of hot dye solution.

Placement print: Also called "engineered print," when the print layout is strategically planned to fall in a specific place on the garment. For example, border prints are often located at the hem or the cuff. This technique is expensive as it results in fabric waste.

Prêt a porter: Also called "ready to wear" or "designer," prêt a porter refers to high-end lines that are machine made and sized with superior fit and finish. Price point is generally less than $1,000; e.g., Thakoon, Peter Som, Missoni, Prada, Versace, St. John, Gucci, Chloe, Donna Karan, Marc Jacobs.

Specs: Often shown alongside flat sketches, specs are the measurements and construction details of a garment that are incorporated into design packages. Specs are essential for sample development as they contain the basic dimensions and instructions for fabrication.

Strike-off: A small patch of fabric printed by the factory to demonstrate and confirm color and pattern quality before proceeding to produce bulk quantities.

Tear sheets: Pages ripped out of magazines that provide inspiration to designers.

Tech pack: Sent to factories to make first samples for approval, tech packs contain detailed flats and specs, artwork layouts, and fabrication instructions. Also called design packages.

Yarn dye: Fabric that is woven or knitted from yarn that was dyed prior to the fabrication of the cloth (e.g. plaid). These are considered to be high quality because yarn-dyes make the fabric resist fading. Often used to describe stripe or jacquard fabrics.

Can't tell your appliqué from your argyle?

We won't let on. Just keep this handy guide close and soon you'll be a true fabric maven.

Appliqué: The art of cutting pieces of one material and applying them to the surface of another in order to embellish a garment.

Bamboo: An eco-friendly fiber often used for jersey products such as T-shirts and socks.

Corduroy: Medium to heavyweight cotton pile fabric. From the French *corde du roi,* meaning "cord of the king," this tough, resilient fabric was first used by the court of French kings.

Crepe: Used to describe fabrics that have a crinkly, rippled, or grained surface. From the French *creper,* which means to crimp. Can be made of various fibers, including wool, cotton, silk, rayon, synthetics, and blends.

Crepe De Chine: A delicate, lightweight crepe often made of silk.

Denim: A cotton textile dyed using indigo; mostly known for its use in blue jeans. Denim is a sturdy twill weave with diagonal ribbing. Originally used for workmen's clothes, it has long since earned its place in the world of high fashion.

Dobby: Woven textile with simple geometric motifs that are created on the fabric during the weaving process.

Eyelet: A series of small and clean finished holes or perforations that are integrated into the pattern of a fabric at regular intervals. These add an airy and beautiful quality.

Facing: A portion of fabric sewn or ironed onto the inside of a pattern piece to add structure and support.

Flannel: Derived from the Welsh word *gwlanen,* which means wool, flannel is made in tightly woven twill or plain weave. It is soft and warm to the touch and is commonly used to make pajamas and bed sheets.

Georgette: A textile traditionally manufactured from silk, though sometimes made of synthetic fabric, georgette is durable, highly absorbent, and can be dyed or printed.

Habotai: A plain weave, lightweight, silk fabric with a soft sheen. Since silk habotai breathes, it is commonly used for linings. Also, its silky texture allows for graceful removing of a garment.

Jacquard: Named for Joseph Marie Jacquard who enabled the loom to create complex patterns in the weave or knit of a textile. Several Jacquard patterns have specific names; e.g., brocade, damask, tapestry.

Jersey: A broad term for a plain knit fabric without a distinct rib. Features small, closely knit stitches. Initially made of wool but now usually made from cotton or a cotton and synthetic blend, jersey fabric was first manufactured on the island of Jersey, near Normandy, France. The fabric is flexible, soft, and insulating, making it a popular choice for the layer worn next to the body. Common uses for jersey fabric include T-shirts and bedding.

Linen: Fibers of the flex plant woven into a fabric that is breezy, resilient, and absorbent. Linen is expensive to manufacture. It can help to whisk perspiration away from the skin, making it popular in hot climates, although it creases easily.

Lyocell: A natural fabric made from vegetable matter or wood pulp. Known for its durability and strength in addition to its eco-friendly manufacturing techniques, Lyocell has a soft hand-feel and a no-crease finish.

Mercerized cotton: Named for John Mercer, this cotton has been immersed in sodium hydroxide to bring out its strength and shine and to increase the dye absorbance. Because the cotton is preshrunk, mercerized cotton also tends not to shrink as much as regular cotton, leading to greater customer satisfaction.

Modal: A processed textile made from the beech tree, which may be used in a blend with cotton, spandex, or other textiles. Modal behaves similarly to cotton, but has greater ability to retain shape when wet, as well as a higher breaking strength. It is very soft and popular for both clothing and household textiles.

Rayon: A manmade fiber derived from processed cellulose, rayon was developed in the 1880s as a cheap substitute for silk. While it drapes well and is easy to dye, rayon tends to deteriorate with age.

Textile Glossary

Garment Encyclopedia

DRESSES	JACKETS	KNITS BASICS	PANTS/SHORTS	SHIRTS	SKIRTS	SWEATERS
Caftan	Biker	Boat	Bootleg	Button-down	A-line	Boyfriend
Empire	Blazer	Cami	Capri	Dolman	Circle	Crew neck
Halter	Bomber	Henley	Five-pocket jeans	Drape	Gathered	Drape front
Jumper	Cape	Polo	High waisted	Mao	Kilt	Grandfather cardigan
Maxi	Denim	Raglan	Leggings	Peasant	Mini	Hoodie
One-shoulder	Military	Scoop	Pleated	Pussy bow	Paneled	Shawl collar
Sheath	Parka	Shell	Sailor	Tunic	Pencil	Shrug
Shirt dress	Pea	Tank	Shorts	Twist	Pleated	Sweater dress
Strapless	Trapeze swing	Turtleneck	Straight leg	Western	Tiered	Sweater set
Wrap	Trench	V-neck	Yoga	Wrap	Wrap	Turtleneck

Taking Accurate Measurements

No matter what size you are, clothes that fit well are always the most flattering. That's why it's important for you to take true and accurate measurements whether you're making clothing for yourself or someone else. Here is not the place to cheat on recording your real waist circumference!

No one likes un-picking seams, so it's well worth taking the bit of time to get this right from the outset. Grab a tailor's tape measure, a retractable tape measure, and a small length (about 40") of elastic.

SOME THINGS TO BEAR IN MIND

- To avoid the dreaded "rubber band" effect, keep the tape measure slack enough that the person being measured can breathe. This way her clothes will skim the body flatteringly instead of cutting into it.
- It's best to wear the type of undergarments that you feel would work with the clothes you're making. For example, wearing a push-up or padded bra, minimizer bra, control top panty, or thong can make a big difference in determining how your finished garment will lay on the body.
- Heel height can dictate your posture and where your hem will fall, so wear the same shoes or heel height you plan on wearing with the outfit while you're being measured.

Note: These instructions are written for someone who is taking her own measurements, but they can just as easily be applied to taking a client's or friend's measurements.

MEASUREMENT CHART

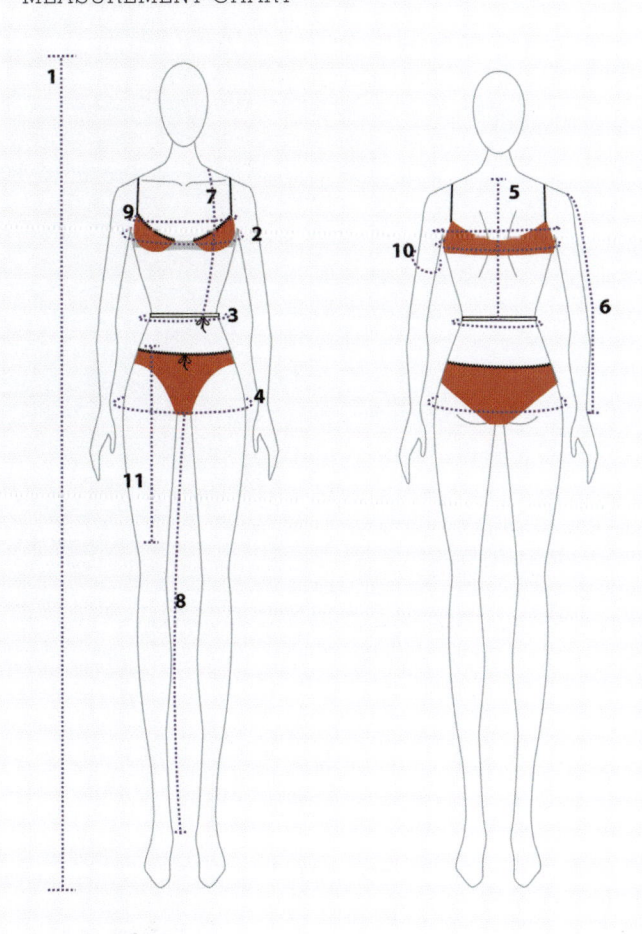

MEASURE

1. **Height:** Stand up straight against a wall and have a friend extend the retractable tape measure from the floor to the top of your head in a straight line running against the wall.

2. **Bust:** Wrap the tailor's tape measure (remember not to squeeze!) around the fullest part of the bust (usually at the nipple line) and straight across your back. Make sure it's not gaping between your shoulder blades; it should be taut and straight.

3. **Waist:** Here's where you need the elastic. Tie the elastic around your waist, and then shift your body from side to side a little until it settles into a comfortable place. This is a great way to locate your "natural" waistline. These days we sometimes refer to our waist as lower than it really is, so this test will ensure that you're measuring around the right place. Now wrap the tailor's tape measure around the elastic to determine your waist measurement. (You can leave the elastic there as it will be useful for steps 4, 5, and 7.)

4. **Hips:** The fullest part of your hips and bottom is usually found 7" to 9" below the natural waistline. Wrap your tailor's tape measure around the fullest part of your hips and straight across your buttocks at the back.

5. **Back Length:** You are going to need a hand for this one, too. Touch your chin to your chest. Now feel the bone jutting out where your neck becomes your spine. You'll need to have your friend measure in a straight line down your spine from this point to your natural waist (where the elastic is sitting).

6. **Sleeve length:** Run your tailor's tape measure from the edge of your shoulder (where the shoulder seam would be) to where you want the sleeve to end.

7. **Front Waist Length:** Locate the point where your shoulder slope becomes your neck, this is called "high point shoulder." Now run your tailor's tape measure from this point, in a straight line over the breast until you hit your waist elastic. (Best to see the Measurement Chart to the left for this one.)

8. **Inseam:** If you're going to take measurements to make pants, slip on a pair of your favorites—if you love the way they fit, they'll be a perfect template for a new pair. Extend the tailor's tape measure over your pants along the inner leg seam, from the crotch down to the desired distance from the floor.

9. **High Bust/Chest:** Extend the tailor's tape measure from one underarm to the other across your front, and complete the circle around the back, keeping the tape taut between shoulder blades.

10. **Upper arm circumference:** Just wrap the tape around the fullest part of the upper arm.

11. **Skirt Length:** Start at the waistline you'll want, which may be lower than your natural waistline, extend the tape measure in a straight line down one leg till you hit the point where you want your skirt to end.

Croquis—it rhymes with "hokey" and is anything but. In fact, a croquis is every fashion designer's secret weapon and it could be yours, too.

Designers, both aspiring and established, sketch over croquis figures to ensure their garments come out proportionally on the first try. Professional designers don't have the time to redraw a template from scratch whenever they want to design a garment. Instead, designers keep a figure on hand that reflects the aesthetic of the brand they work for and use this template as a starting point for all their drafting. Often, they will reuse the same figure, photocopying as necessary, or work with tracing paper and light boxes to layer their designs over the figure again and again. This way, the collections come out cohesive and proportional.

For the designer-in-training, a croquis evens the playing field. Why should you be held back from expressing the great ideas in your head just because you don't have technical figure-drawing training? Often, people say how frustrated they are that something looks fabulous in their mind, but never translates onto paper.

Whether your freehand drawing skills need some work, or your hand isn't as steady as it could be, working on a template provides a rapid-fire way to present your ideas to colleagues, admissions committees, or potential bosses in a polished, professional format. Even if you're not looking to launch a career in fashion, sketching with a croquis can help you share your vision with friends, plan costumes for a school play, or puzzle out your next knitting or sewing project. If you can envision it, using *The Fashion Sketchpad* will help you depict it for all to see. Use these pages to build your skills, hone your personal taste, and refine your design sensibilities. With time, repeatedly working from these guidelines will improve your freehand drawing skills and make the transition from concept to paper a more flowing one.

This sketchpad is packed full of croquis just waiting to be your muse. They come in a variety of on-trend poses that will show your clothes off from every angle. It's like having an arsenal of runway-ready models who are going to rock your looks for the eager audience. You'll notice the figures have fashion industry proportions. This means fantastical dimensions and exaggerated height. Of course, the look of a croquis figure changes to match whatever form is considered in vogue for that time period. Currently, our models are long and lean. They have elongated limbs with very slim hips and a small bust. For better or for worse, our society currently trends toward a beauty ideal featuring more jutting angles than soft curves.

One final trick to tell you: the croquis are printed with a particular ink tone so that they'll disappear when scanned or photocopied, eliminating the evidence of the template completely and letting your designs take center stage.

Happy designing!
We can't wait to see what you come up with.